Freakish Answers to Questions on Animals

M. F. Serene

Published by MASAL Publishing, 2023.

While every precaution has been taken in the preparation of this book, the publisher assumes no responsibility for errors or omissions, or for damages resulting from the use of the information contained herein.

FREAKISH ANSWERS TO QUESTIONS ON ANIMALS

First edition. February 19, 2023.

Copyright © 2023 M. F. Serene.

Written by M. F. Serene.

Table of Contents

To Josephine

Do cows establish
social relationships?

YES, COWS ARE SOCIAL animals and they do establish social relationships with other cows. In fact, cows are known for forming close bonds with their herd mates, often preferring to spend time with specific individuals over others.

Cows have a complex social hierarchy, with dominant and subordinate cows establishing their positions through various social behaviors such as body language, vocalizations, and physical interactions. They form strong bonds with their family members, especially their mothers and calves, and often exhibit social grooming behaviors such as licking and nuzzling.

Research has also shown that cows have the ability to recognize and remember individual cows, even after periods of separation. This suggests that they may have some level of social recognition and memory, which can help them form and maintain social relationships within their herd.

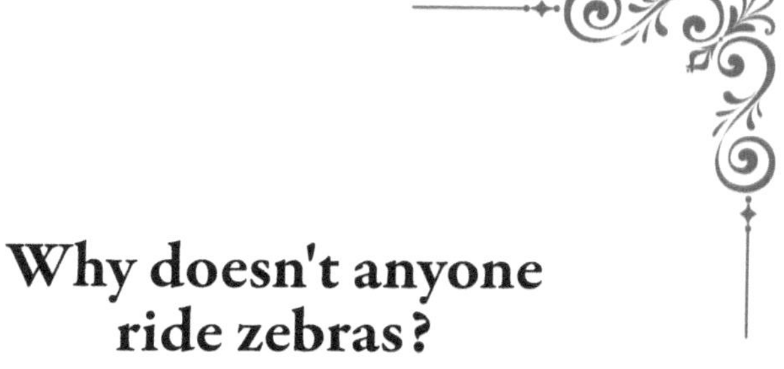

Why doesn't anyone ride zebras?

ZEBRAS ARE NOT COMMONLY used for riding like horses, despite their close genetic relationship to horses, for several reasons.

Firstly, zebras are generally more unpredictable and aggressive than horses, as they are not domesticated animals and are naturally more wary and defensive. They have a strong fight-or-flight response and may be difficult to handle or train for riding.

Secondly, zebras have a different body shape and size than horses, which makes it more difficult to ride them. They have shorter backs, larger hindquarters, and a different gait that makes them less suitable for riding.

Finally, zebras have not been selectively bred for riding, as horses have been over thousands of years, and so they lack the physical and behavioral traits that make horses well-suited for riding.

That being said, there are some examples of people riding zebras, particularly in circuses and shows, but this is not a common practice and is generally not recommended for the average person due to the challenges and risks involved.

Is a giraffe considered an omnivore, carnivore, or herbivore?

A GIRAFFE IS A HERBIVORE, which means it only eats plant-based foods. In the wild, giraffes primarily feed on the leaves, flowers, and fruits of trees and bushes, with acacia leaves being a favorite food. They use their long necks to reach high branches and strip leaves from trees with their prehensile tongues.

Giraffes have a specialized digestive system that allows them to break down tough plant fibers and extract nutrients from their food. They have a four-chambered stomach that helps them ferment their food and extract as much nutrition as possible.

While giraffes are not known to consume meat, they have been observed licking bones and carcasses of dead animals, but this behavior is likely due to a need for additional minerals and not a desire for meat. Overall, giraffes are strictly herbivorous animals.

Is a polar bear really more dangerous than a grizzly bear?

BOTH POLAR BEARS AND grizzly bears are large and powerful predators that are capable of inflicting serious harm to humans. However, polar bears are generally considered more dangerous to humans than grizzly bears, for several reasons.

Firstly, polar bears are marine mammals that are adapted to living in the Arctic and hunting on sea ice, which means that they may be more likely to encounter humans in areas such as hunting camps or on ships in the Arctic region. This increased contact can lead to more frequent interactions and attacks on humans.

Secondly, polar bears are more aggressive than grizzly bears, particularly during the mating season or when they are hungry and in search of food. They are also known to be curious animals that may approach humans out of curiosity, which can increase the risk of an encounter turning violent.

Finally, polar bears are more efficient hunters than grizzly bears and have been known to actively seek out and attack humans as prey. Grizzly bears, on the other hand, are primarily scavengers and are more likely to avoid humans if they can.

That being said, both polar bears and grizzly bears should be treated with caution and respect, and humans should take appropriate safety measures when traveling in areas where these animals are present.

If you switched a chicken egg with that of a duck without the hen noticing, what would happen?

IF YOU SWITCHED A CHICKEN egg with a duck egg and the hen did not notice, then the chicken would likely continue to incubate the egg until it hatched. However, when the egg hatched, a duckling would emerge instead of a chick.

This is because the incubation period and hatching process for ducks and chickens are different. A chicken egg takes about 21 days to hatch, while a duck egg takes about 28 days. Additionally, ducks and chickens have different requirements for humidity and temperature during incubation.

If the hen did not notice the difference and continued to incubate the egg as she normally would, the duckling inside the egg would likely develop normally until it was ready to hatch. When the duckling emerged, the hen may be confused or indifferent to the chick's appearance, as chickens can sometimes adopt and raise young of other species.

However, it's important to note that switching eggs is not recommended as it can disrupt the natural process of incubation and potentially harm the developing embryo. Additionally, it is generally not ethical to interfere with the natural behaviors of animals in this way.

Why do baby animals
suck their trunks?

IT IS COMMON FOR BABY animals to suck on their trunks or other body parts, as it is a natural behavior that helps them to develop and establish important survival skills.

For some animals, such as elephants, sucking on their trunks helps them to learn how to use this appendage for grasping food, water, and other objects. Trunk-sucking behavior also helps young elephants develop their sense of smell, as they are able to suck up different scents from their surroundings.

In other animals, such as primates and some mammals, sucking behaviors are associated with nursing and provide a sense of comfort and security. Sucking on a thumb or finger, for example, can help young animals self-soothe and reduce anxiety.

Sucking behaviors may also be linked to a natural instinct to explore and investigate the world around them. Young animals use their mouths and tongues to taste and touch objects in their environment, and sucking on their own bodies or other objects is one way to engage in this exploratory behavior.

Overall, sucking behavior in baby animals is a natural and important part of their development, helping them to learn important skills and establish a sense of security and comfort as they grow and navigate the world around them.

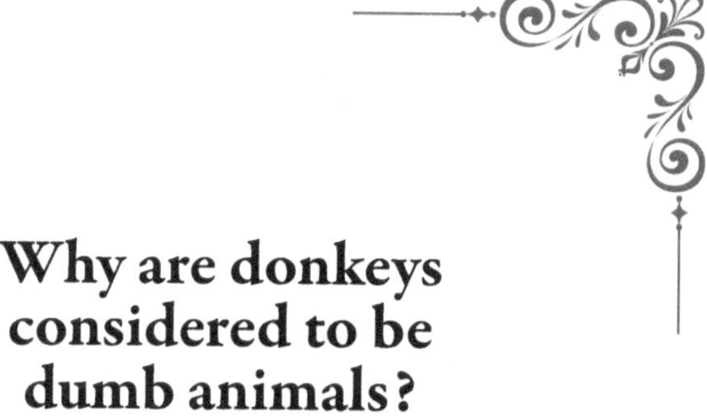

Why are donkeys considered to be dumb animals?

IT IS A COMMON MISCONCEPTION that donkeys are "dumb" animals. While donkeys do have some unique behavioral traits and characteristics, they are not inherently less intelligent than other domesticated animals such as horses, cows, or pigs. In fact, donkeys have been known to exhibit remarkable problem-solving abilities, social intelligence, and other forms of cognitive and emotional intelligence.

One reason why donkeys may be perceived as less intelligent is due to their natural behavior and responses to perceived threats. Donkeys are known for being cautious and hesitant animals, and will often freeze or run away when they encounter a new or potentially dangerous situation. This behavior is actually a survival mechanism, as donkeys are prey animals and need to be constantly vigilant in order to avoid predators. However, this cautious behavior can sometimes be misinterpreted as "stubbornness" or "stupidity" by humans who are not familiar with their natural behavior.

Another reason why donkeys may be considered less intelligent is due to their historical role as beasts of burden. Donkeys have been used for centuries as pack animals and for agricultural work, and were often treated as little more than workhorses. This history of exploitation and mistreatment may have contributed to the perception of donkeys as "dumb" or lacking in intelligence.

However, recent research has shown that donkeys are actually quite intelligent and have a range of cognitive and emotional abilities. For example, donkeys have been shown to be able to recognize other individual donkeys, and to form social bonds with other animals and with humans. They are also capable of learning from past experiences and using that knowledge to solve problems in the future.

Additionally, donkeys have been found to have strong emotional intelligence, and are able to recognize and respond to the emotional states of other animals and humans. They have also been observed engaging in play behavior, which suggests that they have a capacity for joy and social interaction.

In conclusion, the perception that donkeys are "dumb" animals is a stereotype that is not supported by the scientific evidence. While donkeys do have some unique behaviors and traits, they are capable of learning, problem-solving, and emotional intelligence. As with any animal, it is important to understand and respect their natural behavior and characteristics, and to provide them with the appropriate care and treatment.

How many eyes do bees have?

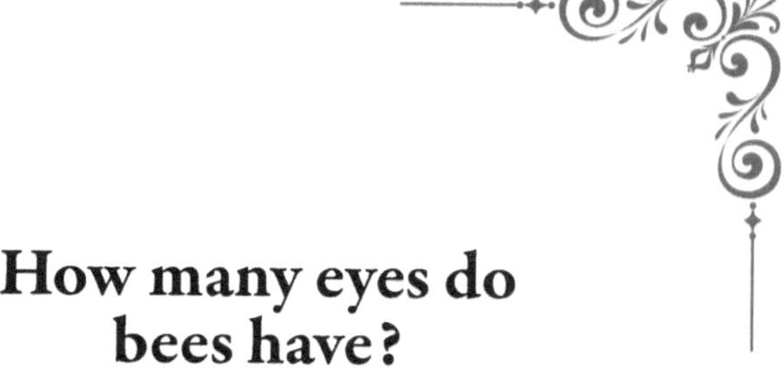

BEES HAVE A UNIQUE and fascinating visual system, with multiple eyes that enable them to see and navigate the world around them in ways that humans can hardly imagine.

To begin with, bees have two large compound eyes, which are located on the sides of their head and are made up of many individual lenses, called ommatidia. The number of ommatidia in a bee's compound eye can vary depending on the species, but is typically in the range of several thousand to tens of thousands.

The ommatidia in a bee's compound eye each contain a photoreceptor cell, which detects light and sends signals to the bee's brain. By combining the signals from many different ommatidia, bees are able to form a complex and detailed image of their surroundings. This allows them to see patterns, colors, and shapes that are invisible to humans, and helps them to navigate and find food.

In addition to their compound eyes, bees also have three smaller eyes, called ocelli, which are located on the top of their head in a triangular formation. The ocelli are simple eyes that contain only one photoreceptor cell each, and are primarily responsible for detecting changes in light intensity and orientation. This allows bees to maintain stability and balance while flying, and to navigate using the position of the sun and other visual cues.

Together, the multiple eyes of a bee form a complex and integrated visual system that allows them to see and interact with their environment in remarkable ways. By leveraging the unique properties of their compound and simple eyes, bees are able to navigate, communicate, and find food in a world that is full of complex and varied stimuli. The study of bee vision continues to be an area of active research, as scientists seek to understand the secrets of this remarkable and vital insect.

Why is pig milk so infrequently consumed by humans?

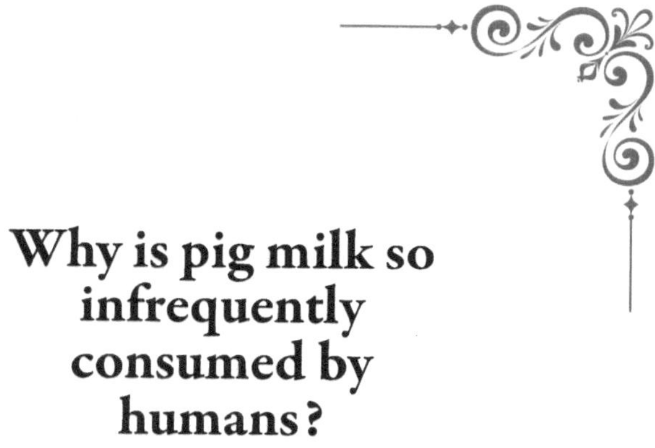

PIG MILK IS AN UNUSUAL and relatively unknown type of milk that is rarely consumed by humans. There are several factors that contribute to the infrequent consumption of pig milk, including the limited availability of pigs as a milk-producing animal, the unique characteristics of pig milk, and the cultural and historical factors that have shaped our attitudes toward pig milk and its consumption.

One of the main reasons why pig milk is not commonly consumed is the fact that pigs are not typically bred or raised for milk production. Unlike cows, goats, or sheep, which have been selectively bred over thousands of years to produce large quantities of milk, pigs have been primarily bred for meat production, with milk production being a secondary consideration. As a result, there are relatively few breeds of pigs that are suitable for milk production, and the quantity and quality of pig milk produced is typically lower than that of other milk-producing animals.

Another factor that contributes to the infrequent consumption of pig milk is the unique characteristics of the milk itself. Pig milk has a high fat content and a strong, gamy flavor that is considered by many to be unappetizing. The milk also contains less lactose than cow's milk, making it a potential option for people who are lactose intolerant, but it also means that the milk may not be as palatable to some people. Additionally, pig milk has a shorter shelf life than other types of milk, making it difficult to store and transport.

Cultural and historical factors have also played a role in shaping our attitudes toward pig milk and its consumption. In many cultures, pigs are seen as dirty or unclean animals, and their milk is therefore considered to be unwholesome or even dangerous to consume. This perception is often linked to religious or cultural beliefs that associate pigs with impurity or unhealthiness. In some cases, the association of pigs with disease or filth may be based on a real or perceived risk of infection or contamination.

Despite these factors, there are some cultures and regions where pig milk is consumed or used in traditional dishes. For example, in some parts of Italy, pig milk is used to make a type of cheese called 'porconero', which is considered a delicacy. In parts of Southeast Asia, pig milk is used in traditional medicine and as a remedy for various ailments. However, these uses of pig milk are relatively rare, and the vast majority of the world's population has little or no experience with consuming or using pig milk.

In conclusion, pig milk is a relatively unknown and infrequently consumed type of milk that is largely the result of the limited availability of pigs as a milk-producing animal, the unique characteristics of pig milk, and the cultural and historical factors that have shaped our attitudes toward pig milk and its consumption. While there are some cultures and regions where pig milk is consumed or used in traditional dishes, it remains a niche product that is unlikely to gain widespread popularity in the near future.

Why can't the antelopes defend themselves against lions?

ANTELOPES ARE A TYPE of herbivorous mammal that are found in a variety of habitats around the world, including grasslands, savannas, and forests. While antelopes have evolved a number of adaptations that allow them to survive in these challenging environments, they are often preyed upon by a variety of predators, including lions, which are among the most successful and feared predators in the animal kingdom. Despite their agility and speed, antelopes are generally not able to defend themselves against lions, and there are several reasons why this is the case.

First, it's important to understand the anatomy and behavior of these two types of animals. Antelopes are typically smaller than lions and lack the physical strength and weaponry to defend themselves against these powerful predators. Antelopes are built for speed and agility, with slender bodies and long, slender legs that allow them to run quickly and change direction rapidly. In contrast, lions are large, muscular predators with powerful jaws, sharp claws, and a variety of other physical adaptations that allow them to capture and kill prey.

Second, lions are apex predators, which means that they are at the top of the food chain and have few natural enemies. This gives them a significant advantage over antelopes and other prey species, which are constantly at risk of being hunted and killed by lions. In addition, lions are social animals that often hunt in groups, which allows them to take down larger and more powerful prey than they would be able to do alone. When lions hunt, they often work together to surround and ambush their prey, making it difficult for antelopes to escape or defend themselves.

Third, antelopes have evolved a number of adaptations that allow them to avoid being eaten by lions, but these adaptations are not foolproof. For example, antelopes have excellent eyesight and hearing, which allows them to detect the presence of predators and flee quickly. However, even the most alert and agile antelopes can fall victim to a surprise attack by a lion, especially if they are hunting in a group or are able to stalk their prey undetected. In addition, many antelopes have evolved a variety of other defenses, such as horns, sharp hooves, and the ability to emit loud alarm calls, but these defenses are often not enough to deter a determined lion.

Finally, it's worth noting that the relationship between antelopes and lions is a complex and dynamic one, with each species constantly adapting to the other in a never-ending struggle for survival. While antelopes may be at a disadvantage when it comes to defending themselves against lions, they have many other adaptations that allow them to thrive in their environments, such as the ability to migrate long distances, to graze on a variety of different plants, and to form herds for protection and social support. Ultimately, the relationship between these two species is a testament to the incredible diversity and complexity of the natural world, and a reminder of the many challenges and opportunities that exist for all living things.

Why are more female turtles born than male turtles?

THE SEX OF TURTLE HATCHLINGS is determined by the temperature at which the eggs are incubated. This process is known as temperature-dependent sex determination (TSD), and it occurs in many reptile species, including turtles. In general, warmer temperatures during incubation produce more female hatchlings, while cooler temperatures produce more males. However, the specific temperature thresholds that result in male or female hatchlings vary between different turtle species.

One reason why more female turtles may be born than males is due to the effects of climate change. As global temperatures continue to rise, the sand or soil in which turtle eggs are laid may become warmer, causing more female hatchlings to be produced. This phenomenon has been observed in several turtle species, including the loggerhead sea turtle, the green sea turtle, and the painted turtle. In some populations of these turtles, the sex ratio has become heavily skewed towards females, which could have serious implications for the survival of these species.

Another factor that can influence the sex of turtle hatchlings is the location of the nest. For example, nests that are closer to the equator may produce more females than nests that are further away, due to the warmer temperatures in these regions. Similarly, nests that are located on the southern-facing slopes of sand dunes may be warmer than nests on northern-facing slopes, resulting in different sex ratios.

In addition to temperature, other environmental factors can also influence the sex of turtle hatchlings. For example, the presence of pollutants, such as plastics or endocrine-disrupting chemicals, may affect the hormones of female turtles, resulting in a higher proportion of female hatchlings. Similarly, the availability of food resources can also impact the sex of hatchlings, with well-fed females more likely to produce female offspring.

It's also worth noting that not all turtle species exhibit temperature-dependent sex determination. Some species have genotypic sex determination, in which the sex of the hatchling is determined by its chromosomes, similar to the way that humans determine sex. However, these species are in the minority, and the majority of turtle species do exhibit TSD.

In conclusion, the sex of turtle hatchlings is primarily determined by the temperature at which the eggs are incubated, with warmer temperatures resulting in more female hatchlings. However, other factors, such as the location of the nest, the presence of pollutants, and the availability of food resources, can also influence the sex ratio of turtle populations. As temperatures continue to rise due to climate change, it is likely that we will see more heavily skewed sex ratios in many turtle species, which could have significant impacts on the health and survival of these animals.

Is extracting wool harmful for sheep?

SHEEP HAVE BEEN BRED for their wool for thousands of years, and in many parts of the world, wool is an important resource for clothing and textiles. However, some people have raised concerns about whether the process of extracting wool is harmful to sheep, both physically and psychologically.

Firstly, it's important to note that sheep need to be shorn regularly for their own welfare. If a sheep is not shorn, its wool will continue to grow, becoming matted and dirty, and potentially leading to health problems such as flystrike (in which flies lay eggs on the wool and their larvae feed on the sheep's flesh). Regular shearing can help prevent these problems and keep sheep healthy.

However, the shearing process itself can be stressful for sheep, especially if it is not done carefully and professionally. Sheep may struggle or become agitated during shearing, which can result in injuries to both the sheep and the shearer. Poorly trained shearers or those in a hurry may inadvertently cut the sheep's skin or leave behind bits of wool that can cause irritation or infection.

In addition, the way that sheep are bred for wool can also have an impact on their welfare. Some breeds of sheep have been selectively bred to produce more and more wool, to the point where they are no longer able to regulate their body temperature effectively. These "wool sheep" may be more prone to heat stress, which can be especially problematic in hot weather. In some cases, they may need to be kept in air-conditioned barns or given special grooming to keep them comfortable.

There have also been concerns about the use of chemicals in the wool industry, such as pesticides to control parasites on sheep or harsh chemicals used in the processing of wool. These chemicals can be harmful not only to sheep, but also to the environment and to people who work with wool.

In recent years, there has been increasing interest in more ethical and sustainable practices in the wool industry, such as using more humane shearing techniques, reducing the use of chemicals, and breeding sheep for wool in a way that is more in line with their natural biology. Some companies and organizations are working to promote these practices and to ensure that sheep are treated with care and respect throughout the wool production process.

In conclusion, while the process of extracting wool from sheep can have some negative impacts on their welfare, it is important to recognize that shearing is a necessary part of caring for sheep, and that many sheep breeds have been selectively bred for wool over many generations. However, it is crucial that shearing is done in a careful and professional manner, and that sheep are not subjected to unnecessary stress or discomfort. By promoting more humane and sustainable practices in the wool industry, we can help ensure that sheep are treated with respect and that we are able to continue enjoying the benefits of this valuable natural resource.

What color skin do polar bears have?

POLAR BEARS HAVE BLACK skin. While this may come as a surprise to many people who associate polar bears with their distinctive white fur, the skin underneath that fur is actually black.

There are a few reasons why polar bears have black skin. One of the most important is that it helps them absorb sunlight more effectively. In the extreme cold of the Arctic, where polar bears live, the sun's rays can be quite weak. However, by having black skin, polar bears are able to absorb as much of that sunlight as possible, which can help keep them warm.

Another reason why polar bears have black skin has to do with their fur. Polar bear fur is actually not white, but rather translucent. Each hair is hollow, and reflects light in a way that makes it appear white. However, the skin underneath that fur is black, which helps to maximize the contrast between the fur and the skin, making the polar bear appear even whiter.

The black skin of polar bears is also important for camouflage. When a polar bear is swimming in the water, the black skin is less visible than white fur would be against the dark water. This allows the polar bear to blend in better with its surroundings, making it less visible to predators and prey.

Finally, it's worth noting that while polar bears have black skin, it is not visible to the naked eye. The fur of a polar bear is so thick and dense that it effectively hides the black skin underneath. However, if you were to shave a polar bear (which is not recommended, as it would be harmful to the animal), you would be able to see the black skin.

In conclusion, polar bears have black skin, which helps them absorb sunlight more effectively, maximizes the contrast between their fur and their skin, and provides effective camouflage. While this may come as a surprise to many people, it is an important adaptation that has helped polar bears survive and thrive in their harsh Arctic environment.

Why are hamsters good pets?

HAMSTERS ARE POPULAR pets for several reasons, and their popularity has only continued to grow over the years. Here are some of the reasons why hamsters are considered to be great pets:

Low maintenance: Hamsters are relatively easy to take care of and require minimal upkeep. They don't need to be walked or bathed, and their cages only need to be cleaned once a week.

Affordable: Compared to other pets, such as dogs or cats, hamsters are relatively inexpensive to own. The cost of food, bedding, and other supplies is relatively low, making them a great option for those on a budget.

Cute and cuddly: Hamsters are small, cute, and furry, which makes them an adorable addition to any household. They are also known for their playful and curious personalities, which can be highly entertaining to watch.

Interactive: Although they don't require much attention, hamsters can be highly interactive pets. They love to play and explore, and they enjoy interacting with their owners. Some hamsters can even be trained to do tricks, such as running through mazes or climbing obstacles.

Quiet: Unlike dogs or cats, hamsters are relatively quiet pets, which makes them a great option for apartment dwellers or those who live in shared spaces.

Lifespan: Hamsters have a relatively short lifespan, usually living for 2-3 years. While this may be a downside for some owners, it also means that they don't require a long-term commitment.

Educational: For children, hamsters can be a great way to learn about responsibility and the importance of taking care of another living being. They can also be a great introduction to the world of pets, which may inspire a lifelong love of animals.

In conclusion, hamsters are great pets for a variety of reasons. They are low maintenance, affordable, cute, interactive, quiet, and can be educational for children. If you're looking for a pet that will bring joy and entertainment to your home without requiring a huge commitment, then a hamster might be the perfect pet for you.

What do leafcutter ants do with the leaves they collect?

LEAFCUTTER ANTS ARE a highly organized and social species of ant that are found in Central and South America. These ants have a unique behavior of collecting and processing leaves, which is what makes them so fascinating.

The primary role of leafcutter ants in their ecosystems is to gather plant material, which they use to cultivate a special type of fungus that serves as their primary source of nutrition. The ants do not eat the leaves themselves, but instead use them to grow the fungus in their underground colonies. This fungus is highly nutritious and contains all of the essential nutrients that the ants need to survive.

The leaf-cutting process itself is an impressive feat of cooperation and division of labor among the ants. The worker ants use their powerful jaws to cut small pieces of leaves from plants, which they then carry back to the nest. Once inside the nest, other ants take over the process of cutting the leaves into even smaller pieces, which are then used to cultivate the fungus.

The ants don't simply collect any type of leaf, either. They are highly selective about the leaves they choose, and prefer leaves that are high in nitrogen and low in lignin. They have also been known to avoid leaves that have been treated with pesticides or other chemicals.

One interesting thing about leafcutter ants is that they have developed a symbiotic relationship with a type of bacteria that grows on their bodies. This bacteria produces an antibiotic substance that helps protect the ants and their fungus from other harmful microbes.

In addition to their important ecological role, leafcutter ants have also captured the imagination of humans. They are a popular subject of study in the field of entomology, and their unique behavior has been featured in numerous documentaries and nature programs.

Are some albatrosses
really lesbians?

ALBATROSSES ARE A TYPE of seabird that are known for their impressive wingspan and their ability to travel long distances over the ocean. They are also known for their unique breeding behavior, which has been the subject of scientific study for many years. In recent years, there has been growing interest in the phenomenon of same-sex pairing among albatrosses, and whether some individuals might be considered "lesbians."

There have been a number of documented cases of female-female pairings among albatrosses, and these pairings are often referred to as "lesbian" relationships. These relationships are not unique to albatrosses, as same-sex pairings have been observed in many other species of birds and animals.

One theory to explain same-sex pairings in animals is that they might be a result of limited options for finding a suitable mate. In the case of albatrosses, finding a mate can be challenging, as they live in remote areas and have a relatively low population density. This can make it difficult for individuals to find a partner of the opposite sex, and might lead them to form bonds with individuals of the same sex.

However, there is also evidence to suggest that same-sex pairing in albatrosses might not be purely a result of limited options for finding a mate. In some cases, female-female pairs have been observed engaging in behaviors that are typically associated with breeding, such as building nests and incubating eggs.

Regardless of the cause of same-sex pairings in albatrosses, it is clear that these relationships can be important for the individuals involved. Studies have shown that same-sex pairs can have similar levels of commitment and dedication to each other as opposite-sex pairs, and can even be more successful at raising chicks than some opposite-sex pairs.

The phenomenon of same-sex pairing in albatrosses is a fascinating and complex topic that continues to be the subject of scientific study. While the term "lesbian" might be used to describe some female-female pairs, it is important to remember that this is a human term that is being applied to a natural phenomenon in the animal kingdom.

How many facial expressions is a horse able to make?

HORSES ARE HIGHLY EXPRESSIVE animals and can communicate a lot through their body language and facial expressions. However, when it comes to the number of facial expressions a horse is able to make, it's hard to give an exact number.

Horses have a very mobile face with many muscles, and they are capable of making a wide range of facial expressions. They use their ears, eyes, nostrils, and mouth to convey different emotions, intentions, and moods. For example, when a horse is happy, it might have its ears forward, its eyes relaxed, and its mouth slightly open. When a horse is angry, its ears will be back, its eyes narrowed, and its mouth tense.

However, there is no definitive answer to how many facial expressions a horse is capable of making because it depends on many factors, including the individual horse's personality, breed, and training. In addition, some researchers suggest that horses have the ability to "smile" and "laugh" in their own way, which further adds to the range of facial expressions they can make.

It's important to note that interpreting a horse's facial expressions can be tricky, and it's not always clear what a horse is trying to communicate. Therefore, it's essential to pay attention to other body language cues as well, such as the horse's posture, tail movement, and vocalizations, to better understand their emotions and intentions.

Are the mosquitos the deadliest animals in the world?

MOSQUITOES ARE ONE of the deadliest animals in the world, but whether they are the deadliest is a matter of debate. There are many factors to consider when determining the deadliest animal, such as the number of deaths caused, the geographic distribution of the animal, and the type of diseases it transmits.

Mosquitoes are known to transmit a variety of deadly diseases, including malaria, dengue fever, Zika virus, chikungunya, and yellow fever. Malaria alone is responsible for over 400,000 deaths per year, mostly in sub-Saharan Africa. In addition, many other mosquito-borne illnesses cause significant morbidity and mortality, particularly in tropical and subtropical regions of the world.

However, other animals are also responsible for a high number of deaths each year. For example, humans kill more than 100 million sharks each year, leading to a decline in shark populations and potentially disrupting marine ecosystems. Snakes are responsible for around 50,000 deaths per year, with the majority of fatalities occurring in Africa and Asia. Dogs, particularly those with rabies, are responsible for over 25,000 deaths per year.

It's worth noting that not all mosquitoes transmit diseases, and the risk of infection varies depending on a variety of factors, including the species of mosquito, the geographic location, and the individual's immune system. Furthermore, efforts to control mosquito populations and prevent the spread of mosquito-borne illnesses have made significant progress in recent years, with the development of effective vaccines and mosquito control strategies.

In conclusion, while mosquitoes are certainly one of the deadliest animals in the world, whether they are the deadliest is a matter of debate. Other animals, such as sharks, snakes, and dogs, are also responsible for significant numbers of deaths each year, and the risk of infection from mosquitoes varies depending on many factors. However, it is clear that the diseases transmitted by mosquitoes are a significant public health challenge, particularly in the developing world, and continued efforts to control mosquito populations and prevent the spread of mosquito-borne illnesses are essential.

Why do wolves howl?

WOLVES ARE HIGHLY SOCIAL animals that rely on communication to coordinate their activities and maintain their complex social structure. Howling is one of the most important ways that wolves communicate with one another, and it can convey a variety of messages depending on the context.

One of the primary reasons that wolves howl is to communicate with other members of their pack. A wolf's howl can be heard for miles, and this makes it an effective way for wolves to locate one another and coordinate their activities. For example, wolves may howl to signal that they are ready to hunt, or to call their packmates back to the den. Howling can also be used to express excitement, joy, or anxiety, as wolves can modulate the pitch and tone of their howls to convey different emotions.

Another reason that wolves howl is to establish and defend their territory. Howling is a way for wolves to let other packs know that an area is occupied, and to warn them not to encroach. This can help prevent conflicts over resources and ensure that the pack has access to food and other necessities. In some cases, wolves may even howl in unison to make their presence known and to assert their dominance in the wild.

Wolves also howl as a form of social bonding. Howling together can strengthen the bonds between pack members and promote cooperation and teamwork. Young wolves may engage in "chorusing" together as a way to practice their vocalizations and bond with one another. Howling can also be a way for wolves to express their identity as members of a pack and to reinforce the social norms and values that define their community.

Finally, wolves may howl simply because it feels good. Howling can be a way for wolves to express themselves and to release pent-up energy and emotion. It can also be a way for wolves to mark their territory and to communicate with potential mates or rivals. Overall, howling is an important part of a wolf's communication system and serves a variety of important functions in their lives.

Why do female lions hunt rather than male lions?

THE QUESTION OF WHY female lions hunt more frequently than their male counterparts is an intriguing one that can be explained through various factors related to lion behavior and biology. Although male lions are generally regarded as the dominant and powerful hunters in a pride, it is actually the females who do most of the hunting, as they possess certain physiological and behavioral adaptations that make them well-suited to this role.

One of the most notable factors that contributes to the hunting behavior of female lions is their smaller size and greater agility. Female lions are typically smaller than males, which allows them to move more quickly and more easily through the bush, tracking and stalking their prey. This smaller size also makes them less conspicuous and easier to hide in the grass, which is an important skill for a successful lion hunter. Additionally, females possess a slightly different skeletal structure than males, which gives them a greater range of motion in their hips and legs, allowing them to run faster and more smoothly over uneven terrain.

Another important factor that contributes to the hunting behavior of female lions is their social structure. Female lions live in prides that are made up of several females and their cubs, along with a few males. These prides are highly structured and hierarchical, with the females at the top of the social order. As such, the females are the ones responsible for hunting and providing food for the pride, while the males are primarily responsible for defending the pride's territory.

It is also worth noting that female lions possess a unique hunting strategy that is well-suited to their strengths and abilities. They often hunt in groups, using a combination of stealth, speed, and teamwork to bring down larger prey such as zebras and wildebeest. Female lions are also known for their patience and persistence, as they will often stalk their prey for hours, waiting for the perfect opportunity to strike.

In contrast, male lions are generally larger and more powerful than females, but they lack the same level of agility and stealth. They are more suited to short bursts of speed and strength, making them better suited for taking down large prey animals such as buffalo or giraffes. However, males are also more likely to scavenge for food or steal kills from other predators, rather than doing their own hunting.

In conclusion, while male lions are certainly impressive and powerful predators, it is actually the females who do most of the hunting in a pride. Their smaller size, agility, and unique hunting strategies make them well-suited to this role, while their social structure and hierarchy within the pride also play a significant role in determining who does the hunting.

Why do pandas do handstands when they pee?

PANDAS ARE KNOWN FOR their quirky and adorable behavior, and one of their most curious habits is performing handstands when they urinate. This behavior has puzzled researchers and animal lovers alike, leading to various theories as to why pandas do this.

One theory is that pandas use handstands as a way to mark their territory. By doing a handstand, pandas can deposit their urine higher up on a tree or other surface, which makes the scent more visible and potent to other pandas in the area. This can help to communicate their presence and dominance to others, and may also deter potential rivals from encroaching on their territory.

Another theory is that handstands help pandas to spread their scent more effectively. By urinating on their hind legs, pandas can spread their scent over a larger area, making it more likely to be detected by other pandas. This can be particularly important for pandas during mating season, when males and females need to find each other to mate.

Yet another theory is that handstands help pandas to avoid stepping in their own urine. Since pandas spend much of their time in trees, they need to be able to climb and jump without slipping or losing their footing. By performing handstands, pandas can deposit their urine higher up on a tree, which reduces the risk of them stepping in it and potentially losing their grip.

Despite these various theories, the exact reason why pandas perform handstands when they pee remains a mystery. It could be that pandas simply enjoy doing it, or that it has some other unknown benefit for them. In any case, this behavior is just one of the many fascinating and endearing traits that make pandas such beloved animals around the world.

What are penguins' marriage routines like?

PENGUINS ARE FAMOUS for their unique and fascinating mating rituals. The process usually begins when the male penguin finds a female he likes, and he'll try to woo her with an impressive display of vocalizations, head-bobbing, and body posturing. If the female is receptive, she will respond by engaging in a mutual head-bobbing dance. Once the pair has formed a bond, they will proceed with the mating process.

Penguins are known to be highly monogamous animals, and they will often mate for life. When it comes to breeding, they generally follow a strict schedule. Penguins typically breed during the winter months, and many species will return to the same breeding ground each year.

Once the female lays her eggs, both parents take turns incubating them, with the males usually taking the first shift. During this time, the male will not leave the nest, and will go without food for several weeks until the chick hatches. Once the chick is born, the parents work together to care for and protect it, with both taking turns foraging for food and keeping the chick warm.

As the chick grows, it will eventually fledge and leave the nest. However, even after the chick has left, the pair will continue to work together to maintain their bond. In fact, penguins have been known to engage in elaborate courtship displays throughout their lives, reaffirming their commitment to each other and strengthening their relationship.

Overall, penguins are incredibly social and devoted animals, and their marriage routines reflect that. From their elaborate courtship displays to their lifelong monogamy and shared parenting responsibilities, penguins are a testament to the power of love and commitment in the animal kingdom.

Why do otters hold hands when going to sleep?

OTTERS ARE OFTEN REGARDED as some of the most playful and social animals, but did you know they also hold hands when they go to sleep? This charming behavior is a demonstration of their close-knit social bonds, and it serves a practical purpose as well.

When otters go to sleep in the water, they hold hands to keep from drifting away from one another. Otters sleep floating on their backs, and they can easily be separated from each other by currents or waves. By holding hands, they create a chain of sorts, with each otter holding on to the next one's paw. This helps them stay close together while they sleep, so they can easily find each other when they wake up.

The hand-holding behavior is not just limited to family groups, either. Otters will often hold hands with other otters in their social group, including friends and siblings. This is just one example of the strong social bonds that exist among these animals.

Another reason why otters hold hands is for grooming. Otters are fastidious groomers, and they will often groom each other's fur to remove dirt and debris. When they hold hands, they can use their free paws to groom themselves or their neighbor's fur. It's like having an extra set of hands to help with personal hygiene!

In addition to being a practical behavior, hand-holding is also a form of communication for otters. When they hold hands, they are sending signals to each other about their intentions and moods. They may also use vocalizations, such as whistles and chirps, to communicate while they hold hands.

Overall, the hand-holding behavior of otters is just one example of the complex social behavior that exists among these charming animals. From holding hands to grooming and communicating, otters have developed a wide range of behaviors to help them live and thrive in their aquatic environments.

Why are some domesticated cats very timid and scared?

THERE ARE NUMEROUS factors that can contribute to a cat's timidity and fearfulness, some of which may be related to their genetics, early life experiences, and current living environment. To understand why some domesticated cats exhibit timid and scared behavior, it is important to delve into the various factors that can influence a cat's personality and disposition.

Firstly, genetics can play a role in a cat's temperament. Certain breeds may be more predisposed to timidity or fearfulness due to their genetic makeup. For example, Siamese cats are known to be very vocal and social, while Persians are typically more laid-back and reserved. Additionally, some cats may have inherited traits from their wild ancestors that make them more cautious or nervous by nature.

Secondly, a cat's early life experiences can have a significant impact on their temperament. Kittens that are not properly socialized during their critical development period (between 2 and 7 weeks of age) may become fearful of people and other animals. Similarly, if a kitten experiences trauma or abuse during this time, they may develop a lifelong fear of certain people or situations. Even kittens that are well-socialized can become timid or fearful if they experience a traumatic event or significant change in their environment later in life.

Thirdly, the current living environment of a cat can also contribute to their timid or scared behavior. Cats that are kept in small or confined spaces with little opportunity for exercise or exploration may become anxious and withdrawn. Similarly, cats that do not have access to proper food, water, or litter box facilities may become stressed and fearful. Additionally, cats that live in households with loud noises, frequent visitors, or other pets may become overwhelmed and retreat into themselves.

It is worth noting that some cats may exhibit timid or scared behavior for no apparent reason, despite being well-socialized, living in a good environment, and having no genetic predisposition towards fearfulness. In such cases, it may be necessary to work with a veterinarian or animal behaviorist to identify the underlying cause of the behavior and develop a plan to address it.

In conclusion, there are numerous factors that can contribute to a cat's timidity and fearfulness, including genetics, early life experiences, and current living environment. By understanding these factors and working to address them, cat owners can help their pets feel more comfortable and secure in their homes.

Can cats taste the air?

CATS HAVE A HIGHLY developed sense of smell, and while they cannot literally "taste" the air, they can gather a great deal of information about their environment and potential prey through their sense of smell. To understand how cats use their sense of smell to perceive their environment, it is important to delve into the biology and anatomy of the feline olfactory system.

The feline olfactory system is much more complex than the human olfactory system. Cats have a special organ in the roof of their mouth called the vomeronasal organ, or Jacobson's organ, which is responsible for detecting pheromones and other chemicals in the air. When a cat encounters an interesting scent, they will often open their mouth slightly and wrinkle their nose in a behavior called the flehmen response, which helps to draw the scent into the vomeronasal organ.

In addition to the vomeronasal organ, cats have a large number of olfactory receptors in their nasal cavity. The average cat has around 200 million olfactory receptors, compared to the average human, who has only around 5 million. These receptors allow cats to detect even the faintest of scents and distinguish between a wide range of different odors.

Cats use their sense of smell to gather information about their environment, identify potential prey, and communicate with other cats. For example, when a cat sniffs the air, they can detect the scent of other animals in the area, including prey animals like mice or birds. They can also detect the scent of other cats, and can use this information to determine whether a particular area has been claimed by another feline.

Furthermore, cats have been known to use their sense of smell to identify human emotions. Studies have shown that cats can detect changes in human body odor that are associated with emotions like fear, happiness, and sadness. This ability may explain why cats are often more attuned to their owners' emotional states than other pets.

While cats cannot literally "taste" the air, their highly developed sense of smell allows them to gather a wealth of information about their environment, potential prey, and other animals in the area. By relying on their sense of smell, cats are able to navigate their surroundings and interact with the world around them in ways that are often beyond our human understanding.

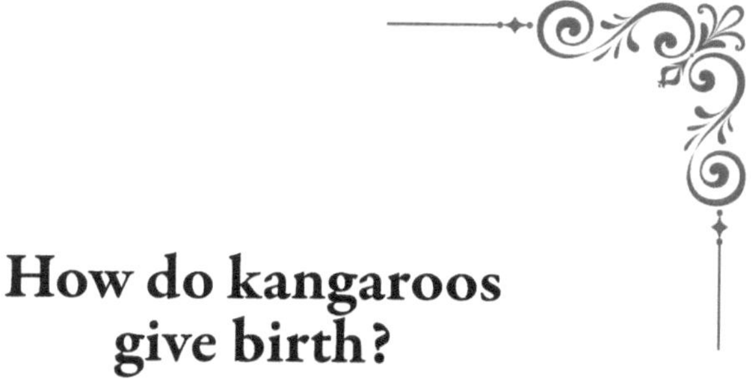

How do kangaroos give birth?

KANGAROOS, LIKE ALL marsupials, have a unique reproductive system that is quite different from that of placental mammals, such as humans. The reproductive process in kangaroos involves a number of distinct stages, including mating, fertilization, gestation, and birth. In order to understand how kangaroos give birth, it is necessary to delve into the intricacies of each of these stages.

Mating in kangaroos typically occurs between January and June, which is their breeding season. During this time, males compete for the attention of females by engaging in boxing matches and other displays of dominance. Once a male has successfully mated with a female, the fertilized egg will develop into an embryo and begin to move down the mother's reproductive tract.

Unlike placental mammals, kangaroos do not have a placenta to nourish the developing embryo. Instead, the embryo remains in a state of suspended animation until it reaches the mother's pouch. The pouch is a specialized structure located on the front of the mother's body, which is used to carry and nurse the young.

Gestation in kangaroos typically lasts around 30-40 days, during which time the embryo develops into a tiny, underdeveloped joey. At the end of this period, the joey is born and immediately climbs into the mother's pouch, where it will continue to develop for several months.

The actual process of giving birth in kangaroos is quite different from that of placental mammals. The newborn joey is not born through the birth canal, but rather emerges from the mother's birth canal as a tiny, hairless, blind, and underdeveloped creature. The joey then uses its front legs to climb up the mother's belly and into the pouch, where it attaches itself to one of the mother's teats.

Once in the pouch, the joey will continue to develop and grow for several months, nursing on the mother's milk and gradually becoming more independent. As it grows, the joey will begin to venture out of the pouch more frequently, but will continue to nurse and seek comfort in the safety of its mother's pouch for up to a year or more.

In conclusion, kangaroos give birth to tiny, underdeveloped joeys, which are born through the mother's birth canal and immediately climb into the mother's pouch. The pouch serves as a specialized structure for carrying and nursing the young, which will continue to develop and grow for several months before becoming more independent. While the reproductive process in kangaroos may be quite different from that of placental mammals, it is perfectly adapted to the unique ecological and environmental conditions in which these animals live.

Does jellyfish have the ability to clone itself?

JELLYFISH ARE FASCINATING creatures that have intrigued scientists and nature enthusiasts for centuries. While there are many species of jellyfish, there are certain types that are known to have the ability to clone themselves, a process known as asexual reproduction.

To understand how jellyfish are able to clone themselves, it is important to first understand their life cycle. Jellyfish start their lives as tiny, free-swimming larvae that eventually settle on a surface and grow into a polyp, which is a stationary, tube-like structure that looks similar to a small sea anemone. The polyp is a crucial stage in the jellyfish life cycle, as it is during this time that the jellyfish is able to reproduce asexually.

To clone itself, the jellyfish polyp undergoes a process called strobilation, in which it begins to develop a series of disc-shaped segments that will eventually break off to become fully-formed jellyfish. Each of these segments is essentially a clone of the original polyp, containing all of the genetic information needed to develop into a mature jellyfish.

Once the segments are fully developed, they break off from the polyp and begin to swim freely in the water, eventually growing into adult jellyfish. This process allows jellyfish to rapidly reproduce and populate an area, making them a successful and adaptable species.

It is important to note that not all jellyfish species have the ability to clone themselves. In fact, there are many different reproductive strategies used by jellyfish, including sexual reproduction, in which a male and female jellyfish release sperm and eggs into the water that eventually fertilize and develop into free-swimming larvae.

In summary, certain types of jellyfish are capable of cloning themselves through a process known as strobilation, which allows the polyp stage to develop a series of genetically identical segments that eventually become fully-formed jellyfish. While not all jellyfish have this ability, it is a fascinating example of the diverse and unique ways that life on Earth is able to reproduce and thrive.

What's the difference between a frog and a toad?

FROGS AND TOADS ARE both amphibians and belong to the order Anura, which means "tailless" in Greek. Despite their similarities, there are some key differences between these two groups of animals that set them apart.

One of the most noticeable differences between frogs and toads is their physical appearance. Frogs typically have smooth, moist skin that is slimy to the touch, while toads have dry, bumpy skin that is covered in warts. Frogs are generally more streamlined in shape, with long, powerful hind legs that are adapted for swimming and leaping. Toads, on the other hand, are more squat and have shorter, stubbier legs that are better suited for walking and hopping short distances.

Another difference between frogs and toads is their habitat preferences. Frogs are often found near bodies of water, such as ponds, lakes, and rivers, where they can breed and lay their eggs in the water. Many species of frogs are also adapted for life in trees and other moist, humid environments. Toads, on the other hand, are typically found in drier habitats, such as grasslands, forests, and deserts. They are better adapted to living on land and can be found in burrows or under rocks during the day.

In terms of behavior, there are some notable differences between frogs and toads as well. Frogs are known for their loud, distinctive calls that they use to attract mates and communicate with one another. They are also more active and agile than toads, and are often seen hopping and jumping around in search of food or shelter. Toads, on the other hand, are generally slower-moving and more sedentary. They are often found sitting still in one spot, waiting for prey to come within range.

Another difference between frogs and toads is their diet. Frogs are generally carnivorous, and feed on a variety of insects, spiders, and other small invertebrates. Some species of frogs are also known to eat other frogs, small fish, and even mice. Toads, on the other hand, are more opportunistic feeders and will eat a wider variety of prey, including insects, worms, and small invertebrates. They are also known to eat toxic insects, such as beetles, and are able to secrete a toxic substance from their skin that deters predators.

Finally, there are some differences in the reproductive strategies of frogs and toads. Frogs typically lay their eggs in large clusters in bodies of water, where they hatch into tadpoles and undergo a metamorphosis into adult frogs. Toads, on the other hand, lay their eggs in long, gelatinous strings that are wrapped around plants in shallow water. The tadpoles that hatch from these eggs are often darker and more heavily pigmented than those of frogs, and they undergo a slower metamorphosis into adult toads.

In conclusion, while frogs and toads may seem quite similar at first glance, there are a number of differences between these two groups of amphibians that set them apart. From their physical appearance and habitat preferences to their behavior, diet, and reproductive strategies, these animals have evolved a variety of unique adaptations that allow them to survive and thrive in different environments.

Why were foxes never domesticated?

FOXES, LIKE MANY OTHER wild animals, have never been fully domesticated in the same way that dogs, cats, and other domesticated animals have. The process of domestication is complex and requires a number of factors to be in place, including the animal's biology, behavior, and the environment in which it lives. While foxes may have some qualities that could potentially make them suitable for domestication, there are several factors that have likely contributed to their lack of domestication.

One of the most significant barriers to fox domestication is their biology. Unlike dogs, which were likely domesticated from wolves over tens of thousands of years, foxes have not been selectively bred for specific traits. This means that they do not have the same range of physical and behavioral variations that dogs do, which has made it more difficult to selectively breed them for domestication. In addition, foxes are not particularly well-suited to living in close proximity to humans. They are naturally skittish and territorial animals, which can make it difficult to keep them in captivity or to train them to live with humans.

Another factor that has likely contributed to the lack of fox domestication is the lack of historical precedent. Dogs were likely domesticated by humans over tens of thousands of years, and their domestication was likely aided by their role as hunting companions and their ability to protect human settlements. Cats were domesticated primarily for their ability to hunt rodents and other pests, as well as for their companionship. Foxes, on the other hand, have never had a clear role in human society, which has likely made it less likely that humans would have attempted to domesticate them.

There are also ethical considerations that have likely contributed to the lack of fox domestication. Domesticating an animal requires significant time and resources, and it may not be ethical to do so simply for the sake of human convenience or curiosity. In addition, there are concerns about the welfare of captive animals, particularly in cases where they are not well-suited to captivity. The process of domesticating a wild animal can also involve significant genetic and behavioral changes, which could have long-term consequences for the animal's health and well-being.

In recent years, there have been some attempts to selectively breed foxes for domestication, particularly in Russia. These experiments have shown some promise, with the resulting foxes showing reduced aggression and increased sociability. However, it is still unclear whether foxes will ever be fully domesticated in the same way that dogs and cats have been. While it is certainly possible that humans could find a way to selectively breed foxes for domestication, there are a number of biological, historical, and ethical factors that will need to be taken into account if this is to happen.

Do animals have blood types like humans?

YES, ANIMALS DO HAVE blood types like humans. In fact, the concept of blood types is not unique to humans and has been observed in a wide variety of animal species. The most well-known blood typing system is the ABO blood group system, which was first discovered in humans in the early 20th century. However, there are several other blood typing systems that have been identified in animals, including the MNS, Duffy, Kidd, and Kell systems.

Blood types are determined by the presence or absence of certain molecules, called antigens, on the surface of red blood cells. In humans, the ABO blood group system is based on the presence or absence of the A and B antigens, as well as the presence of antibodies against the missing antigen in the recipient's blood. Animals have similar antigens on their red blood cells that determine their blood type. For example, dogs have DEA (Dog Erythrocyte Antigen) blood types, while cats have A, B, and AB blood types.

Blood typing is important in veterinary medicine, particularly in transfusion medicine. Like humans, animals may require blood transfusions due to injury, surgery, or disease. In order to ensure a successful transfusion, it is important to match the blood type of the donor and recipient. Giving a recipient blood that is incompatible with their own blood type can cause a severe reaction, similar to a transfusion reaction in humans.

In addition to transfusion medicine, blood typing can also be useful in determining the parentage of animals in breeding programs. By analyzing the blood types of potential parents and offspring, breeders can determine the likelihood of certain blood types being passed on to future generations.

Overall, while the concept of blood types is often associated with humans, it is a fundamental aspect of biology that is present in many animal species. Understanding blood typing in animals is crucial for the development of effective veterinary medicine and breeding programs.

Do dogs really have three eyelids? Why?

YES, DOGS DO HAVE THREE eyelids, and the reason for this is rooted in their evolution and anatomy. To understand this, we must first look at the structure of the canine eye.

The canine eye is composed of several parts, including the cornea, iris, pupil, lens, and retina. These structures work together to focus light onto the retina, where it is converted into electrical signals that are sent to the brain for interpretation.

The three eyelids of the dog are called the upper eyelid, lower eyelid, and nictitating membrane, which is also known as the third eyelid. The upper and lower eyelids are similar to those of humans and function to protect and lubricate the eye. They are able to blink and close completely to provide full coverage and protection to the eye.

The nictitating membrane, on the other hand, is a translucent or transparent third eyelid that is located in the inner corner of the eye. This eyelid can be moved across the surface of the eye to protect it from foreign objects, and to spread tears and other secretions across the cornea for lubrication and cleaning purposes. It also contains lymphoid tissue, which is part of the immune system and helps to fight infections and other foreign invaders.

The presence of the nictitating membrane in dogs is thought to have evolved as a protective adaptation. Unlike humans, dogs are often exposed to dust, dirt, and other foreign objects while running, playing, and exploring their environments. The nictitating membrane provides an additional layer of protection to the eye, helping to prevent injury and infection.

In addition to its protective functions, the nictitating membrane also plays a role in regulating the amount of light that enters the eye. By moving across the surface of the eye, it can help to reduce glare and adjust the amount of light that is allowed into the eye.

Overall, the three eyelids of the dog are a unique and important feature of their anatomy. They provide essential protection and lubrication to the eye, as well as immune support and light regulation. While they may seem unusual to us as humans, they are a critical component of the canine visual system and an important part of their evolutionary history.

Why do cats hate belly rubs?

THE IDEA THAT CATS universally hate belly rubs is a common misconception. While some cats do not enjoy having their bellies touched, others may actively seek out belly rubs and enjoy them. However, there are several reasons why many cats may be sensitive or averse to having their bellies touched, and these reasons are rooted in both their evolutionary history and their individual personalities.

First, it is important to understand that the belly is a vulnerable area for cats. In the wild, cats are predators and are constantly on guard against potential threats. Their bellies are soft and exposed, making them a prime target for attack by other animals, including predators and prey. As a result, many cats have developed a natural instinct to protect their bellies and may become defensive or anxious when this area is touched.

Additionally, cats are highly sensitive creatures and may have different preferences when it comes to physical touch. While some cats enjoy being petted and cuddled, others may find certain types of touch overstimulating or uncomfortable. This can be influenced by a range of factors, including their individual temperament, their past experiences with touch, and their current mood.

Another factor that may influence a cat's response to belly rubs is the context in which they are offered. If a cat is feeling stressed or anxious, they may be more likely to respond negatively to touch, including belly rubs. Conversely, if a cat is feeling relaxed and comfortable, they may be more open to receiving physical affection, including belly rubs.

It is also worth noting that the way in which a person touches a cat's belly can make a difference in how the cat responds. Cats are very particular about their personal space and may become uncomfortable if they feel their boundaries are being violated. It is important to approach a cat slowly and gently, and to respect their signals if they indicate that they are not interested in being touched.

Overall, the idea that cats universally hate belly rubs is a myth. While some cats may not enjoy this type of touch, others may actively seek it out and find it pleasurable. However, there are several reasons why many cats may be sensitive or averse to having their bellies touched, including their natural instinct to protect this vulnerable area, their individual temperament and preferences, and the context in which the touch is offered. By understanding and respecting a cat's individual needs and preferences, we can build stronger bonds with our feline friends and provide them with the love and care they need to thrive.

Why are flamingos pink?

FLAMINGOS ARE A TYPE of wading bird known for their distinctive pink plumage, which is often cited as one of the most striking and recognizable features of these majestic animals. But why exactly are flamingos pink? The answer to this question is complex, multifaceted, and deeply rooted in the biology and behavior of these fascinating creatures.

To begin with, it is important to note that the pink coloration of flamingos is not a universal trait across all species or subspecies of this bird. Rather, it is most commonly observed in the greater flamingo, a species of bird found throughout much of Africa, southern Europe, and southwestern Asia. While other species of flamingos may exhibit some degree of pink or reddish coloration, the greater flamingo is by far the most well-known for its distinctive hue.

So, what causes this pink coloration in the greater flamingo? The answer, in short, is pigments. Specifically, the pink color of flamingos is largely the result of a group of pigments known as carotenoids, which are organic compounds that are found in a wide variety of plants and animals. In flamingos, these carotenoids are derived from the birds' diet, which consists largely of small aquatic organisms such as shrimp, algae, and other invertebrates that are rich in these pigments.

When flamingos consume these carotenoid-rich organisms, the pigments are absorbed into the birds' bloodstream and eventually make their way to the feather follicles, where they are incorporated into the growing feathers. Over time, this accumulation of carotenoids in the feathers gives flamingos their characteristic pink coloration.

It is worth noting, however, that the precise shade of pink can vary depending on a number of factors, including the age, sex, and health of the individual bird, as well as environmental factors such as the availability and quality of food sources. In general, though, the more carotenoids a flamingo consumes, the more intense and vibrant its pink coloration is likely to be.

Beyond their striking appearance, the pink coloration of flamingos also serves a number of important functions. For example, it is believed that the coloration may play a role in social signaling, with brighter, more colorful individuals being more attractive to potential mates. Additionally, the coloration may serve as a form of camouflage, helping the birds blend in with their surroundings and avoid predators.

In conclusion, while the question of why flamingos are pink may seem straightforward at first glance, the answer is actually quite complex and multifaceted, reflecting the intricate interplay between biology, behavior, and environment. From the role of carotenoid pigments in creating the distinctive hue of their feathers, to the potential social and ecological functions of this coloration, the pinkness of flamingos is a fascinating topic that continues to capture the imagination of scientists and laypeople alike.

How can you reliably distinguish ravens from crows?

THE DISTINCTION BETWEEN ravens and crows can be challenging, as they are both members of the Corvidae family, known for their intelligence and adaptability. However, there are a few key differences that can help distinguish these two birds from each other, ranging from physical characteristics to behavioral patterns and vocalizations.

First and foremost, size can be a helpful indicator. Ravens are generally larger than crows, with wingspans up to four feet and a weight of up to 4 pounds, whereas crows typically have a wingspan of around two feet and weigh around 1 pound. However, this size difference can be challenging to discern in the field, particularly if the birds are not observed side-by-side.

Another physical difference to note is the shape of the tail. Ravens have wedge-shaped tails that are longer and more pointed, while crows have fan-shaped tails that are shorter and more rounded. Additionally, ravens tend to have heavier, thicker beaks than crows, which are more slender.

Behaviorally, ravens are often more solitary than crows, and can be observed flying or perching alone or in pairs, whereas crows are more social and often seen in larger flocks. Ravens are also known for their playful behavior, and can be observed engaging in aerial acrobatics, sliding down snow banks, and playing with objects such as sticks and rocks. Crows, on the other hand, are more commonly observed foraging in groups and calling to one another.

Vocalizations can also be a useful tool for distinguishing between ravens and crows. Ravens have a much deeper and more resonant call, often described as a deep croak or a low, guttural "gronk." Crows, on the other hand, have a higher-pitched and more nasal call, often described as a "caw-caw" or a "ka-ka-ka."

Another key distinction between the two birds is their range and habitat. Ravens are more commonly found in mountainous or wilderness areas, while crows are more adaptable and can be found in a wider range of habitats, including suburban and urban areas. Ravens are also more commonly found in the western part of North America, while crows are found throughout the continent.

Overall, while distinguishing between ravens and crows can be challenging, careful observation of their physical characteristics, behavior, and vocalizations can help to reliably differentiate between these two fascinating and intelligent bird species.

About the Author

M.F. Serene is a book editor who works tirelessly behind the scenes to bring the best literary works to the reading public. His real identity is a closely guarded secret, known only to a select few in the publishing industry. M.F. Serene is, in fact, a pen name that he has chosen to maintain his privacy.

Born and raised in a small town, M.F. Serene developed a love for reading and writing at an early age. He spent his youth immersed in books, and his passion for literature only grew stronger as he got older. Despite his love of writing, M.F. Serene realized that his true calling was in editing and publishing, where he could help other writers achieve their dreams of becoming published authors.

After completing his education, M.F. Serene moved to New York City to begin his career in the publishing industry. He quickly made a name for himself as a skilled editor with an unerring eye for detail and an intuitive sense of what makes a great book. Over the years, he has worked with a wide variety of writers, from established bestsellers to up-and-coming debut authors.

Despite his success, M.F. Serene has always maintained a low profile, preferring to keep his real identity a secret. He is known to be reclusive and rarely makes public appearances, preferring to communicate with his clients and colleagues through email and other digital channels.

Despite his secretive nature, M.F. Serene is highly respected in the publishing industry, and his insights and opinions are highly valued by those who know him. He is a true master of his craft, and his commitment to helping writers achieve their best work has earned him a place among the most respected book editors in the business.

About the Publisher

Welcome to our publishing house! We are a team of passionate and dedicated professionals who are committed to bringing fresh, compelling, and thought-provoking literature to the world. Our focus is on publishing innovative, high-quality works that inspire, challenge, and delight readers of all ages and backgrounds.

Whether you're a lover of fiction, non-fiction, poetry, or any other genre, we have something for you. Our diverse catalog features emerging voices, established authors, and everything in between. We are proud to offer a platform for both established and emerging writers to showcase their work and reach a wider audience.

At our publishing house, we believe that books have the power to transform lives, spark conversations, and create connections. We are dedicated to creating books that not only entertain, but also challenge and inspire our readers to think deeply about the world around them. We are excited to be a part of the vibrant and ever-changing world of publishing, and we look forward to sharing our passion for books with you.

Thank you for choosing our books, and we hope that you find something that captures your imagination and inspires you to keep reading.

www.ingramcontent.com/pod-product-compliance
Lightning Source LLC
Chambersburg PA
CBHW051430250726
48656CB00020B/1863